# THE TRULY HEALTHY COFFEE COOKBOOK

A Complete Beginners Guide To Mouth-

Watering, Easy And Healthy Coffee Recipes To

Delight The Senses, Nourish Your Body And

Boost Health

## Luigi Russo

1

# *Let's start!*

# Table of Contents

**Use Your Favorite Coffee Machines To Brew For Cooking**

**71 Delicious Recipes**

# Use Your Favorite Coffee Machines To Brew For Cooking

If you love your cup of java then you love to try some foods that use coffee as an ingredient.

Usually coffee is used in dessert, but it isn't just used for sweet foods. Coffee is also used in sauces for meat, in spicy chili, and even for certain kinds of pot roasts.

Grinding your own beans or buying them freshly ground is the best way to ensure that your coffee flavors will come out well in your food. Use filtered water in your coffee maker brew your coffee right before cooking to make sure it is the freshest it can be. You should also be aware then when using coffee to cook, it is usually prepared a lot stronger than how you would drink it. Here's some great recipes to try in your kitchen.

**Meatloaf Sauce with Coffee**

Outside of Australia this traditional sauce is gaining popularity. It's delicious and simple. Start by adding a tablespoon of instant coffee to ¼ cup of filtered water, ½ cup of ketchup, and ¼ cup of dry red wine, add some Worcestershire sauce to taste, two tablespoons of vinegar, a spoonful of margarine, and finally two tablespoons of lemon juice and a hint of brown sugar.

Let your meat cook for 30 minutes before adding the sauce and then add your sauce and cook for 45 more minutes at 190C or 375F.

**Espresso Flavored Brownies**

For the chocolate and coffee lover, this is the best recipe out there!

In a sauce pan combine a cup of sugar, ¼ teaspoon salt, and a stick and half of buttern and heat. Now add a teaspoon of vanilla, four ounces of chopped up semi-sweet chocolate, and stir entire mixture until its melted. You can now add a tablespoon of your favorite ground dark-roast or you can add two teaspoons of espresso granules for an interesting change.

Now that it's all mixed up then pour it into a bowl to allow it to cool. Add three eggs while the mixture is still warm and a cup of flour. Pour the whole thing into a baking pan and bake for 30 minutes.

**Black Russian Cake**

Using a store-bought dark chocolate cake mix you can add one cup of veggie oil, one packaged of instant pudding (chocolate of course), four eggs, ½ cup crème de cacao, and for the final touch add Russian coffee. Use 1 oz of vodka, ½ oz of Kahlua, and 5 oz of hot black coffee to make this mixture.

Beat all the ingredients together and use a tube pan to bake at 350F or 177C for 45 minutes.

If you want to get creative try using coffee in all kinds of recipes from cookies to ice cream! Try Kahlua which is made from coffee to enhance all kinds of desserts.

Make your own coffee syrup using a cup of sugar and a cup of extra strength Colombian. Boil them together in a pan on the stove and let the sugar dissolve. Simmer at a lower temperature and then allow it to cool. A great treat over ice cream!

No matter what your favorite coffee machines are, give these inventive recipes a try!

# 285 Delicious Recipes

# Mexican Coffee Balls

## Ingredients

- 1 (9 ounce) package chocolate wafer cookies, crushed
- 1/2 pound ground almonds 1/3 cup unsweetened cocoa powder
- 1/4 cup white sugar
- 2 tablespoons instant coffee powder
- 1/3 cup coffee flavored liqueur 1/2 cup light corn syrup
- 1/4 cup white sugar
- 2 teaspoons ground cinnamon

## Directions

In a large bowl, mix chocolate wafer crumbs, ground blanched almonds, unsweetened cocoa powder, and 1/4 cup sugar. Dissolve instant coffee in coffee liqueur and stir into crumb mixture with corn syrup. Shape into 1/4 inch balls and roll in cinnamon sugar.

To make cinnamon sugar, combine 1/4 cup sugar with 2 teaspoons cinnamon. Store in refrigerator.

# Quick N' Easy Coffee Cake or Muffins

## Ingredients

- 4 cups all-purpose flour 2/3 cup sugar
- 2 (.25 ounce) envelopes
- Fleischmann's® RapidRise Yeast
- 1 1/2 teaspoons salt
- 1/2 cup water
- 1 cup milk
- 6 tablespoons butter OR margarine
- 2 eggs
- Sugar Nut Topping:
- 1/4 cup butter OR margarine
- 1 cup brown sugar
- 1 cup chopped walnuts

## Directions

Combine 1 cup flour, sugar, undissolved yeast and salt in a large mixing bowl. Heat water, milk and butter until very warm (120 to 130 degrees F).

Gradually add to dry ingredients; beat 2 minutes at medium speed of electric mixer, scraping bowl occasionally. Add eggs and 1/2 cup flour; beat 2 minutes at high speed, scraping bowl occasionally. Stir in remaining flour to make a stiff batter.

Turn into 2 greased 8 or 9-inch square pans. Or, to make muffins, fill 24 greased muffin tins half full. Sprinkle evenly with Sugar-Nut Topping (see directions below). Cover; let rise in warm, draft-free place until doubled in size, about 1 hour.

Bake at 350 degrees F for 20 to 25 minutes or until done. Remove from pans; cool on wire racks.Sugar-Nut Topping: Combine butter

and brown sugar with a pastry blender or two knives until mixture resembles coarse crumbs.
Stir in chopped walnuts.

# Apple Coffee Cake

## Ingredients

- 1/2 cup butter flavored shortening
- 1 cup sugar
- 2 eggs
- 1 teaspoon vanilla extract
- 2 cups all-purpose flour
- 1 teaspoon baking powder
- 1 teaspoon baking soda 1/2 teaspoon salt
- 1 cup sour cream
- 1 3/4 cups chopped, peeled tart apples
  TOPPING:
- 3/4 cup packed brown sugar
- 1 teaspoon ground cinnamon
- 2 tablespoons cold butter or margarine
- 1/2 cup chopped walnuts

## Directions

In a mixing bowl, cream shortening and sugar. Add eggs and vanilla; mix well.

Combine flour, baking powder, baking soda and salt; add to the creamed mixture alternately with sour cream. Stir in apples. Transfer to two greased 8-in. square baking dishes. For topping, combine brown sugar and cinnamon.
Cut in butter until crumbly. Stir in nuts; sprinkle over batter. Bake at 350 degrees F for 30-35 minutes or until a toothpick inserted near the center comes out clean. Cool completely.

Cover and freeze for up to 6 months. Thaw overnight in the refrigerator.

# Easy Streusel Coffee Cake

## Ingredients

- 1 (18.25 ounce) package yellow cake mix
- 1 (3.5 ounce) package instant vanilla pudding mix
- 1/3 cup vegetable oil
- 4 eggs
- 1 cup plain yogurt
- 1 tablespoon unsweetened cocoa powder
- 1/2 cup chopped walnuts
- 1 teaspoon ground cinnamon

## Directions

Beat yellow cake mix, instant vanilla pudding mix, oil, eggs and yogurt together until no lumps remain.In a separate bowl  mix cocoa, chopped nuts, and cinnamon together.

Spray a large bundt pan with cooking spray  and put 1/2 of batter in pan.  Sprinkle streusel mix over batter and top streusel with remaining batter.

Bake at 350 degrees F (175 degrees C) for 50 minutes. Cool for 15 minutes and take out of pan.

# Strawberry Rhubarb Coffee Cake

## Ingredients

- 2/3 cup sugar
- 1/3 cup cornstarch
- 2 cups chopped fresh or frozen rhubarb
- 1 (10 ounce) package frozen sweetened sliced strawberries, thawed
- 2 tablespoons lemon juice CAKE:
- 3 cups all-purpose flour
- 1 cup sugar
- 1 teaspoon baking powder
- 1/2 teaspoon baking soda
- 1 cup cold butter
- 2 eggs
- 1 cup buttermilk
- 1 teaspoon vanilla extract

TOPPING:
- 3/4 cup sugar
- 1/2 cup all-purpose flour 1/4 cup cold butter

## Directions

In a saucepan, combine sugar and cornstarch; stir in rhubarb and strawberries. Bring to a boil over medium heat; cook for 2 minutes or until thickened. Remove from the heat; stir in lemon juice. Cool.For cake,in a large bowl, combine flour, sugar, baking powder and baking soda in a large bowl.

Cut in butter until mixture resembles coarse crumbs. Beat the eggs, buttermilk and vanilla; stir in crumb mixture just until moistened.Spoon two-thirds of the batter into a greased 13-in. x 9-in. x 2-in. baking dish.

Spoon cooled filling over batter.

Top with remaining batter. For topping, combine sugar and flour. Cut in butter until mixture resembles coarse crumbs; sprinkle over batter.

Bake at 350 degrees F for 45-50 minutes or until golden brown. Cool on a wire rack.

# Dutch Coffee Custard (Hopjesvla)

## Ingredients

- 4 tablespoons custard powder
- 1 5/8 cups whole milk, divided 5/8 cup white sugar
- 7 tablespoons strong brewed coffee
- 1 egg yolk
- 1 egg white

## Directions

In a small bowl, mix together the custard powder and 1/2 cup of the milk; set aside. Sprinkle the sugar into a saucepan over medium heat.

When the sugar begins to caramelize, add the remaining milk and coffee to the pan, and bring to a boil. At this stage, the caramel will become very crusty. Reduce heat to low, and cook until the sugar dissolves, about 5 minutes. Stir in the custard powder mixture, and cook, stirring until the custard thickens.

Remove from heat, and whisk in the egg yolk. In a clean glass or metal bowl, whip the egg white until soft peaks form. Fold the egg white carefully into the custard mixture. Transfer to a serving dish and refrigerate until firm.

# Coconut Coffee Mousse

## Ingredients

- 1 (8 ounce) container frozen whipped topping, thawed
- 2 tablespoons coffee flavored liqueur
- 1/4 cup flaked coconut

## Directions

Fold coffee liqueur and coconut into whipped topping until well combined. Pour into 8x8 inch baking dish and freeze 4 hours, until firm.

# Springtime Coffee Cake

## Ingredients

- 2 cups fresh or frozen unsweetened strawberries
- 1 1/2 cups diced fresh or frozen rhubarb
- 3/4 cup sugar
- 3 tablespoons cornstarch
- 3 tablespoons cold water CAKE:
- 1 1/2 cups all-purpose flour 3/4 cup sugar
- 1 teaspoon ground cinnamon 1/2 teaspoon ground nutmeg ½ teaspoon salt
- 1/2 teaspoon baking powder 1/2 teaspoon baking soda
- 3/4 cup cold butter or margarine
- 2 eggs
- 3/4 cup buttermilk
- 1/2 teaspoon almond extract

TOPPING:

- 1/2 cup sugar
- 1/2 teaspoon ground cinnamon
- 1 tablespoon cold butter
- 1/2 cup chopped walnuts

## Directions

In a saucepan, combine strawberries, rhubarb and sugar; let stand for 15 minutes. Combine cornstarch and water; stir into the fruit mixture. Bring to a boil over medium heat, stirring constantly. Cook and stir for 2 minutes. Cool to room temperature.

Combine flour, sugar, cinnamon, nutmeg, salt, baking powder and baking soda; cut in butter until crumbly. In a small mixing bowl, beat eggs, buttermilk and extract; add to flour mixture and mix well.

Spread half of the batter into a greased 9-in. square baking pan. Carefully spoon the fruit mixture on top. Spoon remaining batter over fruit mixture.

For topping, combine sugar and cinnamon; cut in butter until crumbly. Stir in walnuts. Sprinkle over batter.
Bake at 350 degrees F for 40-45 minutes or until a wooden pick inserted near the center comes out clean.

# Coffee and Doughnuts Ice Cream

## Ingredients

- 3 day-old glazed doughnuts, cut into 8 pieces
- 1 cup cold, strong, brewed coffee 1/2 cup sugar
- 2 cups heavy cream
- 1 (14 ounce) can sweetened condensed milk
- 1/2 cup milk
- 1 teaspoon vanilla extract

## Directions

Place the doughnut pieces in a single layer in the bottom of a shallow dish. Pour just enough of the coffee over the doughnuts so the liquid is completely absorbedby the doughnuts.

Put the dish in the freezer. Mix the remaining coffee with the sugar, cream, sweetened condensed milk, milk, and vanilla in a bowl; stir. Pour the mixture into an ice cream maker and freeze according to manufacturer's directions until the ice cream cycle is completed.

Fold the frozen doughnuts into the mixture; transfer ice cream to a one- or two-quart lidded plastic container; cover surface with plastic wrap and seal. Ripen in the freezer for at least 12 hours.

# Raspberry Almond Coffeecake

## Ingredients

- 1 cup fresh raspberries
- 3 tablespoons brown sugar
- 1 cup all-purpose flour 1/3 cup white sugar
- 1/2 teaspoon baking powder 1/4 teaspoon baking soda 1/8 teaspoon salt
- 1/2 cup sour cream
- 2 tablespoons butter, melted
- 1 teaspoon vanilla extract 1 egg
- 1/4 cup sliced almonds
- 1/4 cup sifted confectioners' sugar
- 1 teaspoon milk 1/4 teaspoon vanilla extract

## Directions

Preheat oven to 350 degrees F (175 degrees C). Spray an 8 inch round cake pan with cooking spray.mCombine raspberries and brown sugar in a bowl. Set aside.mIn a large bowl, combine flour, sugar, baking soda, baking powder, and salt.

Combine sour cream, butter or margarine, 1 teaspoon vanilla, and egg, and add to flour mixture. Stir just until moist. Spoon 2/3 of the batter into the prepared pan.

Spread raspberry mixture evenly over the batter. Spoon remaining batter over raspberry mixture. Top with almonds. Bake for 40 minutes, or until a wooden pick inserted in center comes out clean. Let cool for 10 minutes on a wire rack.

Combine confectioners' sugar, milk, and 1/4 teaspoon vanilla. Stir well. Drizzle glaze over cake. Serve warm or at room temperature.

# Coffee Chip Cookies

## Ingredients

- 1 cup shortening
- 2 cups packed brown sugar
- 2 eggs
- 1 cup boiling water
- 2 tablespoons instant coffee granules
- 4 cups all-purpose flour
- 2 teaspoons baking powder
- 1 teaspoon baking soda
- 4 cups semisweet chocolate chips

## Directions

In a mixing bowl, cream shortening and brown sugar. Add eggs, one at a time, beating well after each addition. Combine water and coffee; set aside. Combine the flour, baking powder and baking soda; add to creamed mixture alternately with coffee. Stir in the chocolate chips. Refrigerate for 1 hour.

Drop dough by rounded tablespoonfuls 2 in. apart onto greased baking sheets.

Bake at 350 degrees F for 10-12 minutes or until golden around the edges. Remove to wire racks.

# Coffee Nut Torte

## Ingredients

- 1/2 cup butter or margarine
- 1 cup sugar
- 3 eggs, separated
- 1/2 cup all-purpose flour
- 2 teaspoons baking powder
- 2 cups finely ground graham cracker crumbs
- 1 cup cold, strong, brewed coffee
- 1 teaspoon vanilla extract 3/4 cup chopped nuts
  FILLING:
- 1 (3.4 ounce) package instant vanilla pudding mix
- 1 1/4 cups milk
- 1 teaspoon instant coffee granules 1/2 cup heavy cream, whipped

## Directions

In a large mixing, bowl, cream butter and sugar. Add egg yolks; beat until light. Sift together flour and baking powder; add crumbs.
Add alternately with coffee to creamed mixture, beating well until smooth. Stir in vanilla and nuts. In another bowl, beat egg whites until stiff; fold into batter.

Pour into two 8-in. round waxed paper-lined baking pans. Bake at 350 degrees F for 30-35 minutes. Cool completely. For filling, prepared pudding with milk and coffee; chill. Fold in cream.
Split each cake layer and spread with filling.

# Sesame Coffee Cake

## Ingredients

- 1/2 cup vegetable oil 3/4 cup honey
- 3/4 cup tahini
- 1 1/2 teaspoons baking powder
- 1 1/2 teaspoons ground nutmeg
- 2 cups all-purpose flour
- 1/2 cup sesame seeds
- 1 cup water

## Directions

Preheat oven to 350 degrees F (175 degrees C).

Lightly grease a tube pan or a 9 x 13 inch baking pan. In a medium bowl combine oil, honey, tahini, baking powder and nutmeg; mix well. Stir in flour, sesame seeds and water.

Pour into prepared pan.

Bake in preheated oven for 35 to 40 minutes, or until a toothpick inserted into the cake comes out clean.

# Cranberry Crumble Coffee Cake

## Ingredients

- 1/4 cup chopped almonds
- 1 cup sugar
- 1/2 cup butter, softened
- 1 teaspoon vanilla extract
- 2 eggs
- 2 cups all-purpose flour
- 1 1/4 teaspoons baking powder 1/2 teaspoon baking soda
- 1/4 teaspoon salt
- 1 cup sour cream
- 1 cup whole berry cranberry sauce
  TOPPING:
- 1/4 cup all-purpose flour 1/4 cup sugar
- 1/4 cup chopped almonds
- 1/4 teaspoon vanilla extract
- 2 tablespoons cold butter

## Directions

Sprinkle almonds over the bottom of a greased 9-in. springform pan; set aside. In a mixing bowl, cream the sugar, butter and vanilla; beat on medium for 1-2 minutes. Add eggs, one at a time, beating well after each addition.

Combine dry ingredients; add to batter alternately with sour cream. Mix well. Spread 3 cups over almonds. Spoon cranberry sauce over batter. Top with remaining batter.

For topping, combine flour, sugar, almonds and vanilla; cut in butter until crumbly. Sprinkle over batter.

Bake at 350 degrees F for 70-75 minutes or until a toothpick inserted near the center comes out clean.

Cool in pan on a wire rack for 15 minutes; remove sides of pan. Serve warm.

# Creamy Ice Coffee

## Ingredients

- 1 1/2 quarts brewed coffee, room temperature
- 1 cup milk
- 1 cup half-and-half cream 1/3 cup white sugar
- 1 teaspoon vanilla extract
- 2 tablespoons creme de cacao

## Directions

In a pitcher, combine cooled coffee, milk and half-and-half. Stir in sugar, vanilla and creme de cacao.

Chill in refrigerator until ready to serve.

# Newfoundland Coffee

## Ingredients

- 1 fluid ounce dark rum
- 1 fluid ounce coffee flavored liqueur
- 8 fluid ounces hot brewed coffee
- 1/2 fluid ounce Irish cream liqueur
- 1 maraschino cherry

## Directions

Measure rum and coffee liqueur into a coffee mug.
Pour in hot coffee. Top with Irish cream, and garnish with a cherry.

# Mexican-Style Coffee

## Ingredients

- 4 fluid ounces hot brewed coffee
- 1 fluid ounce coffee liqueur
- 1 fluid ounce tequila
- 1 tablespoon whipped topping (optional)
- 1 pinch ground cinnamon, for garnish (optional)
- 1 pinch cocoa powder, for garnish (optional)

## Directions

Pour the coffee into a mug. Stir in the coffee liqueur and tequila. Garnish with whipped topping, cinnamon, and cocoa powder.

# Pear Coffee Cake

## Ingredients

- 2 cups sugar
- 1 1/2 cups vegetable oil
- 3 eggs
- 3 cups all-purpose flour
- 1 teaspoon ground cinnamon
- 1 teaspoon salt
- 1 teaspoon baking soda
- 2 teaspoons vanilla extract
- 2 cups flaked coconut
- 1 cup chopped dates
- 3 cups chopped peeled pears
- 1 cup pecans, chopped

## Directions

In a mixing bowl, cream together sugar and oil. Add eggs, one at a time, beating well after each addition. Sift together flour, cinnamon, salt and baking soda; add to creamed mixture.

Add vanilla. Bay hand, stir in coconut, dates, pears and pecans (batter will be thick). Spoon into a greased and floured fluted tube pan. Bake at 325 degrees F for 1-1/2 to 2 hours or until cake tests done.

Cool on rack until cake comes away from sides of pan; remove from pan to a wire rack to cool completely.

# Aunt Dee Dee's Apple Coffee Cake

## Ingredients

- 1 (21 ounce) can apple pie filling
- 2 teaspoons ground cinnamon
- 3 cups all-purpose flour
- 1 cup white sugar
- 1 1/2 cups milk
- 1/2 cup butter, softened
- 3 teaspoons baking powder
- 1 teaspoon salt
- 3 eggs
- 1/4 cup packed brown sugar 1/4 cup chopped walnuts
- 2 tablespoons butter, melted
- 3/4 cup confectioners' sugar
- 1 tablespoon butter, melted
- 3/4 teaspoon vanilla extract
- 2 1/2 teaspoons hot water

## Directions

Preheat oven to 350 degrees F (175 degrees C). Grease a 9x13 pan. Mix pie filling and cinnamon, set aside.Beat flour, white sugar, milk, 1/2 cup softened butter, baking powder, salt and eggs in mixing bowl on low speed for 30 seconds.

Bea on medium speed for 2 minutes.Pour half of the batter into prepared pan. Spoon half of the pie filling over the batter. Spread remaining cake batter over pie filling and top with the remaining half of the pie filling.

Mix brown sugar and nuts together and sprinkle over top of cake. Drizzle with 2 tablespoons melted butter. Bake at 350 degrees F (175 degrees C) for 45 to 55 minutes.

Allow cake to cool 20 minutes.Combine confectioners sugar, 1 tablespoon butter, 3/4 teaspoon vanilla, 2 to 3 teaspoons hot water. Beat until smooth.
Drizzle over cake.

# Irish Coffee

## Ingredients

- 1 (1.5 fluid ounce) jigger Irish cream liqueur
- 1 (1.5 fluid ounce) jigger Irish whiskey
- 1 cup hot brewed coffee
- 1 tablespoon whipped cream
- 1 dash ground nutmeg

## Directions

In a coffee mug, combine Irish cream and Irish whiskey. Fill mug with coffee.
Top with a dab of whipped cream and a dash of nutmeg.

# Sweet Sausage Coffee Ring

## Ingredients

- 1 cup water
- 1 cup golden raisins
- 1 pound bulk pork sausage
- 1 1/2 cups sugar
- 1 1/2 cups packed brown sugar 2 egg
- 1 cup chopped pecans
- 3 cups all-purpose flour
- 1 teaspoon baking powder
- 1 teaspoon baking soda
- 1 teaspoon ground ginger
- 1 teaspoon pumpkin pie spice
- 1 cup strong brewed coffee, room temperature
  GLAZE:
- 1/2 cup confectioners' sugar
- 2 teaspoons milk
- 1/4 teaspoon vanilla extract

## Directions

In a saucepan, bring water to a boil; reduce heat. Add raisins. Cover and simmer for 5 minutes; drain and set aside. Crumble sausage into a large bowl. Add sugars and eggs; mix well. Stir in pecans and reserved raisins. Combine the flour, baking powder, baking soda, ginger and pie spice; add to sausage mixture alternately with coffee.

Transfer to a greased and floured 10-in. tube pan. Bake at 350 degrees F for 1-1/4 to 1-1/2 hours or until a toothpick inserted near the center comes out clean. Cool for 10 minutes before removing from pan to a wire rack.

Combine glaze ingredients; drizzle over cooled bread. Refrigerate leftovers.

# Coffee Frosting

## Ingredients

- 1 teaspoon instant coffee granules 1/4 cup milk
- 1/4 cup unsweetened cocoa powder
- 6 tablespoons butter
- 1 1/2 teaspoons vanilla extract
- 5 cups confectioners' sugar

## Directions

Mix together; instant coffee or leftover coffee, milk, cocoa powder, butter or margarine, vanilla extract, and confectioners' sugar until of spreading consistency.

Makes more than enough to frost a 13x9 inch sheet cake.

# Candy Bar Coffee Cake

## Ingredients

- 2 cups all-purpose flour
- 1 cup packed brown sugar 1/2 cup sugar
- 1/2 cup cold butter or margarine
- 1 teaspoon baking soda
- 1 teaspoon salt 1 egg
- 1 cup buttermilk
- 1 teaspoon vanilla extract
- 3 (1.4 ounce) bars Heath candy bars, crushed
- 1 cup chopped pecans

## Directions

In a large bowl, combine the flour and sugars; cut in butter until the mixture resembles coarse crumbs. Set aside 1/2 cup for topping. To the remaining crumb mixture, add baking soda and salt.

Beat egg, buttermilk and vanilla; add to the crumb mixture and mix well.

Pour into a greased 11-in. x 7-in. x 2-in. baking pan. Combine the candy bars, pecans and reserved crumb mixture; sprinkle over the top.

Bake at 350 degrees for 40 minutes or until a toothpick inserted near the center comes out clean.

# Honey Comb Coffee Cake

## Ingredients

- 1 3/4 cups all-purpose flour 1/2 cup white sugar
- 1/2 cup unsalted butter 1/3 cup milk
- 2 eggs
- 2 teaspoons baking powder 1/2 teaspoon almond extract 1/2 teaspoon orange extract 1/2 cup unsalted butter
- 1/2 cup chopped pecans 1/4 cup white sugar
- 1/2 teaspoon ground nutmeg
- 1 tablespoon milk
- 1/2 teaspoon orange extract 1/4 cup honey

## Directions

Preheat oven to 350 degrees F (175 degrees C); grease and flour a 9 inch square baking pan. Combine flour, 1/2 cup sugar, 1/2 cup butter or margarine, 1/3 cup milk, eggs, baking powder, 1/2 teaspoon orange extract , and almond extract until well mixed.

Spread batter into prepared pan.
To Make Topping:  In a heavy 2 quart saucepan combine 1/2 cup butter or margarine, pecans, 1/4 cup sugar, honey, nutmeg, 1 tablespoon milk, and 1/2 teaspoon orange extract.

Cook over medium heat, stirring occasionally, until mixture comes to a full boil. Continue cooking, stirring occasionally, for 2 or 3 minutes. Pour topping evenly over coffee cake.

Bake 22 to 27 minutes, or until wooden pick inserted in center comes out clean.

# Lemon Coffee Cake

## Ingrediets

- 1 1/4 cups sugar, divided 3/4 cup vegetable oil
- 4 eggs
- 2 cups all-purpose flour
- 1 teaspoon baking powder 1/2 teaspoon salt
- 1 (15.75 ounce) can lemon pie filling
- 1 1/2 teaspoons ground cinnamon

## Directions

In a mixing bowl, combine 1 cup sugar and oil; mix well. Add eggs; beat until light and lemon-colored.

Combine flour, baking powder and salt; add to the egg mixture and mix well. Pour half into a greased 13-in. x 9-in. x 2-in. baking dish. Spread pie filling over batter. Top with remaining sugar; sprinkle over the top.

Bake at 350 degrees F for 30 minutes or until a toothpick comes out clean. Cool on a wire rack.

# Cream Cheese Coffee Cake

## Ingredients

- 1/2 cup butter, softened
- 1 cup sugar
- 3 eggs
- 1 teaspoon vanilla extract
- 2 cups all-purpose flour
- 1 teaspoon baking powder
- 1 teaspoon baking soda 1/4 teaspoon salt
- 1 cup sour cream FILLING:
- 2 (3 ounce) packages cream cheese
- 2 tablespoons confectioners' sugar
- 2 tablespoons lemon juice
  CINNAMON-NUT TOPPING:
- 1/4 cup finely chopped pecans
- 2 tablespoons sugar
- 1/2 teaspoon ground cinnamon

## Directions

In a large mixing bowl, cream butter and sugar. Add eggs and vanilla; beat well. Combine the flour, baking powder, baking soda and salt; add to creamed mixture alternately with sour cream. Set batter aside. In a small mixing bowl, beat cream cheese, confectioners' sugar and lemon juice until smooth. Spoon half of the batter into agreased and floured 10-in. tube pan. Top with filling and remaining batter. Combine topping ingredients; sprinkle over batter.

Bake at 350 degrees F for 30-35 minutes or until a toothpick inserted near the center comes out clean. Cool for 10 minutes before removing form pan to wire rack.

# Rated G Mexican Coffee

## Ingredients

- 6 cups water
- 1/4 cup brown sugar
- 1 (3 inch) cinnamon stick
- 1 whole clove
- 1/2 cup ground coffee beans 1/2 teaspoon vanilla
- 1/4 cup chocolate syrup
- 1 cup whipped cream

## Directions

Bring the water, sugar, cinnamon, and clove to a boil in a large saucepan over high heat. Stir until the sugar has dissolved, then remove from the heat, stir in the coffee grounds, cover, and steep for 5 minutes.

Stir in the vanilla and chocolate syrup, then strain through several layers of cheesecloth to remove the coffee grounds and spices.

Serve with a dollop of whipped cream.

# Candy Bar Coffee Cake

## Ingredients

- 2 cups all-purpose flour
- 1 cup packed brown sugar 1/2 cup sugar
- 1/2 cup cold butter or margarine
- 1 teaspoon baking soda
- 1 teaspoon salt 1 egg
- 1 cup buttermilk
- 1 teaspoon vanilla extract
- 3 (1.4 ounce) bars Heath candy bars, crushed
- 1 cup chopped pecans

## Directions

In a large bowl, combine flour and sugars; cut in butter until mixture resembles coarse crumbs. Set aside 1/2 cup for topping.

To the remaining crumb mixture, add baking soda and salt. Beat egg, buttermilk and vanilla; add to the crumb mixture and mix well. Pour into a greased 11-in. x 7-in. x 2-in. baking pan.

Combine candy bars, pecans and reserved crumb mixture; sprinkle over the top.
Bake at 350 degrees F for 40 minutes or until a toothpick inserted near the center comes out clean.

# Pumpkin Coffee Cake

## Ingredients

TOPPING:
- 1/4 cup packed brown sugar 1/4 cup sugar
- 1/2 teaspoon ground cinnamon
- 2 tablespoons cold butter or margarine
- 1/2 cup chopped pecans CAKE:
- 1/2 cup butter or margarine, softened
- 1 cup sugar
- 2 eggs
- 1 cup sour cream
- 1/2 cup canned or cooked pumpkin
- 1 teaspoon vanilla extract
- 2 cups all-purpose flour
- 1 teaspoon baking soda
- 1 teaspoon baking powder 1/2 teaspoon pumpkin pie spice 1/4 teaspoon salt

## Directions

In a small bowl, combine sugars and cinnamon. Cut in the butter until mixture resembles coarse crumbs. Stir in pecans; set aside. In a mixing bowl, cream butter and sugar.

Add eggs, one at a time, beating well after each addition. Combine the sour cream, pumpkin and vanilla; mix well. Combine dry ingredients; add to creamed mixture alternately with sour cream mixture.
Beat on low just until blended. Spread the batter into two greased and floured 8-in. round cake pans. Sprinkle with topping.

Bake at 325 degrees F for 40-50 minutes or until a toothpick inserted near the center comes out clean.

# Apple Coffee Cake

## Ingredients

- 1/2 cup butter, softened
- 1 cup sugar
- 3 eggs
- 3 cups all-purpose flour
- 3 teaspoons baking powder
- 1 teaspoon salt
- 1 1/2 cups milk
- 1 (21 ounce) can apple pie filling
- 2 teaspoons ground cinnamon TOPPING:
- 1/2 cup chopped walnuts
- 1/4 cup packed brown sugar
- 2 tablespoons butter, melted GLAZE:
- 3/4 cup confectioners' sugar
- 1 tablespoon butter, softened 3/4 teaspoon vanilla extract
- 2 teaspoons water

## Directions

In a large mixing bowl, cream butter and sugar. Beat in eggs. Combine the flour, baking powder and salt; add to creamed mixture alternately with milk. Pour half into a greased 13-in.x 9-in.x 2-in. baking dish. Combine pie filling and cinnamon; spoon over batter.

Drop remaining batter over filling; spread gently.Combine topping ingredients; sprinkle over batter. Bake at 350 degrees F for 40-45 minutes or until a toothpick inserted near the center comes out clean.

Cool on a wire rack. Combine glazeingredients; drizzle over warm or cooled coffee cake.

# Cinnamon Coffee Bars

## Ingredients

- 1/3 cup butter, softened
- 1 cup packed brown sugar 1 egg
- 1/3 cup hot, strong brewed coffee
- 1 1/2 cups all-purpose flour
- 1 teaspoon baking powder
- 1 teaspoon ground cinnamon 1/4 teaspoon baking soda
- 1/4 teaspoon salt
- 1 cup semisweet chocolate chips 1/2 cup chopped walnuts GLAZE:
- 3/4 cup confectioners' sugar
- 1/4 teaspoon vanilla extract
- 3 teaspoons milk

## Directions

In a large mixing bowl, cream butter and brown sugar. Add egg; beat well. Beat in coffee. Combine the flour, baking powder, cinnamon, baking soda and salt; gradually add to creamed mixture. Stir in chocolate chips and walnuts. Spread into a well-greased 8-in. square baking dish.

Bake at 350 degrees F for 30-35 minutes or until a toothpick inserted near the center comes out clean. In a small bowl, combine the confectioners' sugar, vanilla and enough milk to achieve a glaze consistency.

Drizzle over warm bars. Cool completely on a wire rack before cutting.

# Coffee Liqueur II

## Ingredients

- 6 cups water
- 1/2 cup instant coffee granules
- 6 cups white sugar
- 1/2 cup vanilla extract 1/2 gallon vodka

## Directions

In a 4 quart saucepan, bring to a boil the water, instant coffee and sugar.

Simmer for 2 hours, then allow to cool. When cool, add vanilla and vodka.

# Raisin Buttermilk Coffee Cake

## Ingredients

- 1 cup packed brown sugar
- 1 cup chopped nuts
- 1/3 cup butter or margarine, melted
- 2 tablespoons all-purpose flour
- 4 teaspoons ground cinnamon BATTER:
- 1/2 cup butter or margarine, softened
- 1 1/2 cups sugar
- 2 eggs
- 3 cups all-purpose flour
- 4 teaspoons baking powder 1/2 teaspoon salt
- 2 cups buttermilk
- **1 cup raisins**

## Directions

In a bowl, combine the first five ingredients until mixture resembles coarse crumbs; set aside. In a mixing bowl, cream butter and sugar. Add eggs, one at a time, beating well after each addition.

Combine the dry ingredients; add to creamed mixture alternately withbuttermilk. Stir in raisins. Spread half of the batter into a greased 13-in. x 9-in. x 2-in. baking pan. Sprinkle with half of the crumb mixture. Carefully spread with remaining batter and sprinkle with remaining crumb mixture.

Bake at 350 degrees F for 35-40 minutes or until a toothpick inserted near the center comes out clean.

# Light Cinnamon Coffee Cake

## Ingredients

- 1/2 cup fat-free milk 1/4 cup canola oil
- 1/4 cup egg substitute
- 3/4 cup all-purpose flour
- 3/4 cup whole wheat flour 1/2 cup sugar
- 2 teaspoons baking powder 1/2 teaspoon salt
  TOPPING:
- 1/2 cup packed brown sugar 1/2 cup chopped walnuts
- 1 tablespoon all-purpose flour
- 1 teaspoon ground cinnamon
- 1 teaspoon melted margarine

## Directions

In a mixing bowl, beat milk, oil and egg substitute. Combine the dry ingredients; add to milk mixture and beat until smooth. Spoon into 8-in. square baking pan coated with nonstick cooking spray.

Combine the topping ingredients; sprinkle over batter. Bake at 375 degrees F for 25-28 minutes or until a toothpick inserted near the center comes out clean.
Cool on a wire rack.

# Thai Coffee

## Ingredients

- 2 tablespoons ground coffee beans
- 1/4 teaspoon ground cardamom water
- 2 tablespoons sweetened condensed milk

## Directions

Place coffee and cardamom in the filter of your coffee machine. Place enough water to make 2 cups of coffee in the machine. Turn on the coffee machine.

Pour brewed coffee into 2 coffee cups, and stir 1 tablespoon sweetened condensed milk into each cup.
Serve.

# Apricot Coffee Cake

## Ingredients

- 1 (.25 ounce) package active dry yeast
- 1/4 cup warm water (105 degrees to 115 degrees)
- 3/4 cup warm milk (110 to 115 degrees F)
- 1 egg
- 1/2 cup butter or margarine, softened
- 4 cups all-purpose flour 1/2 cup sugar
- 1/2 teaspoon salt
  APRICOT FILLING:
- 12 ounces dried apricots 3/4 cup water
- 3/4 cup sugar
- 1/4 teaspoon ground cinnamon GLAZE:
- 1/2 cup confectioners' sugar
- 1 teaspoon milk
- 1/2 teaspoon butter or margarine, softened
- 1/2 teaspoon vanilla extract

## Directions

In a large mixing bowl, dissolve yeast in warm water. Add warm milk, egg and butter; mix. Add 2-1/2 cups flour, sugar and salt; beat until smooth.

Add enough remaining flour to form a soft dough. Turn onto floured surface; knead until smooth and elastic, about 6-8 minutes. Place in a greased bowl, turning once to grease top.
Cover and let rise in a warm place until doubled, about 1 hour. For filling, combine apricots and water in a saucepan. Cover and simmer for 30 minutes. Cool 10 minutes.

Pour into a blender; process at high speed until smooth. Stir in sugar and cinnamon; set aside. Punch dough down. Divide in half and roll each half into a 15-in. x 12-in. rectangle. Place on a greased baking sheet. Spread half of the filling in a 15-in. x 4-in. strip down center of dough. With a sharp knife, cut dough on each side of apricot filling into 1-in. wide strips. Fold strips alternately across filling to give braided effect.

Repeat with remaining dough and filling. Cover and let rise until doubled, about 30 minutes. Bake at 375 degrees F for 20 minutes or until golden brown. Cool on wire racks for 15 minutes.
Combine glaze ingredients; drizzle over warm coffee cakes. Serve warm or allow to cool completely.

# Coffee Flavored Liqueur II

## Ingredients

- 3 cups white sugar
- 4 cups water
- 1/4 cup instant coffee granules
- 1 (750 milliliter) bottle vodka
- 1 vanilla bean

## Directions

In a saucepan, combine sugar, water and instant coffee. Bring to a boil, then let simmer gently for 1 hour. Remove from heat, and cool completely.

When mixture is cool, Stir in vodka. Place vanilla bean in bottle and fill with coffee/vodka mixture. Allow liqueur to set for 4 to 6 weeks after preparation.

# Coffee Shop Corn Muffins

## Ingredients

- 1 1/4 cups cornmeal
- 1 cup all-purpose flour
- 1/3 cup packed brown sugar 1/3 cup sugar
- 1 teaspoon baking soda 1/2 teaspoon salt
- 1 egg
- 1 cup buttermilk
- 3/4 cup vegetable oil

## Directions

In a bowl, combine cornmeal, flour, sugars, baking soda and salt. In another bowl, beat egg, buttermilk and oil; stir into dry ingredients just until moistened.
Fill greased or paper-lined muffin cups three-fourths full.

Bake at 425 degrees F for 12-15 minutes or until muffins test done. Cool in pan for 10 minutes before removing to a wire rack.

# Country Apple Coffee Cake

## Ingredients

- 2 medium tart apples, peeled and chopped
- 1 (12 ounce) package refrigerated buttermilk biscuits
- 1 egg
- 1/3 cup corn syrup
- 1/3 cup packed brown sugar
- 1 tablespoon butter or margarine, softened
- 1/2 teaspoon ground cinnamon 1/2 cup chopped pecans GLAZE:
- 1/3 cup confectioners' sugar
- 1/4 teaspoon vanilla extract
- 1 teaspoon milk

## Directions

Place 1-1/2 cups apples in a greased 9-in. round baking pan. Separate biscuits into 10 pieces; cut each biscuit into quarters.

Place over apples with point side up. Top with remaining apples. In a mixing bowl, combine egg corn syrup, brown sugar, butter and cinnamon. Stir in pecans. Spoon over apples.

Bake at 350 degrees F for 30-35 minutes or until biscuits are browned. For glaze, combine confectioners' sugar, vanilla and enough milk to achieve desired consistency. Drizzle over warm coffee cake.
Serve immediately.

# Cranberry Swirl Coffee Cake

## Ingredients

- 1/2 cup butter
- 1 cup white sugar
- 2 eggs
- 1 teaspoon almond extract
- 2 cups all-purpose flour
- 1 teaspoon baking powder
- 1 teaspoon baking soda 1/2 teaspoon salt
- 1 cup sour cream
- 1 (8 ounce) can whole cranberry sauce

## Directions

Preheat oven to 350 degrees F (175 degrees C). Grease and flour one 9 or 10 inch tube pan. In a large bowl, cream together the butter and sugar until light and fluffy.

Beat in the eggs one at a time, then stir in the almond extract. Combine the flour, baking powder, baking soda, and salt; stir into the creamed mixture alternately with the sour cream. Pour 1/3 of the batter into the prepared tube pan. Swirl 1/2 of the cranberry sauce into the batter.

Repeat, ending with the batter on top. Bake 55 minutes in the preheated oven, until golden brown.

# Chocolate Coffee Bread

## Ingredients

- 1 1/3 cups water
- 1/3 cup cocoa powder
- 1 1/3 cups bread flour
- 1 1/3 cups whole wheat flour
- 3 tablespoons dry milk powder
- 1 1/2 teaspoons salt
- 1 1/2 tablespoons vegetable oil
- 3 tablespoons honey
- 2 1/4 teaspoons active dry yeast 1/2 cup semisweet chocolate chips
- 2 envelopes instant mocha cappuccino mix

## Directions

Place all ingredients (except chocolate chips and mocha mix) in the pan of the bread machine in the order recommended by the manufacturer.

Select Basic Bread cycle; press Start. If your machine has a Fruit setting, add the chocolate chips and mocha mix at the signal, or about 5 minutes before the kneading cycle has finished.

# Sour Cream Streusel Coffee Cake

## Ingredients

- 3 tablespoons dry bread crumbs
- 3 1/4 cups all-purpose flour 1/2 teaspoon baking soda ¼ teaspoon salt
- 3/4 cup butter
- 2 1/2 cups white sugar
- 3 eggs
- 2 teaspoons vanilla extract
- 1 (8 ounce) container sour cream
- 1/4 cup brown sugar
- 1 tablespoon ground cinnamon 1/4 cup chopped pecans
- 1 cup confectioners' sugar
- 2 tablespoons milk

## Directions

Preheat oven to 350 degrees F (175 degrees C). Coat a 10 inch tube pan with non-stick cooking spray and dust with bread crumbs. Sift together the flour, baking soda and salt.

Set aside. In a small bowl, mix streusel ingredients - brown sugar, cinnamon and chopped pecans; set aside. In a large bowl, cream together the butter and white sugar until light and fluffy. Beat in the eggs one at a time, then stir in the vanilla. Beat in the flour mixture alternately with the sour cream, mixing just until incorporated.

Spoon half of the batter into prepared pan. Sprinkle half of the streusel mixture over the batter. Repeat with remaining batter and streusel mixture.

Bake in the preheated oven for 60 to 70 minutes, or until a toothpick inserted into the center of the cake comes out clean. Let cool in pan for

10 minutes, then turn out onto a wire rack and cool completely. In a small bowl, combine confectioners' sugar with milk, a tablespoon at a time, until desired consistency is achieved.

Drizzle over the cake.

# Apple Coffee Cake With Brown Sugar Sauce

## Ingredients

- 2 apples - peeled, cored and chopped
- 2 1/2 cups all-purpose flour
- 1 1/2 cups packed brown sugar 3/4 cup butter, softened
- 1 cup chopped walnuts, toasted
- 1 teaspoon baking soda
- 1 teaspoon ground cinnamon 1/2 teaspoon salt
- 1 egg
- 3/4 cup sour cream
- 1 teaspoon vanilla extract

## Directions

Preheat oven to 375 degrees F (190 degrees C). Butter a 9 inch round cake pan or 9 1/2 inch springform pan.

Using a fork, work flour with brown sugar and butter in a large bowl until crumbly. Stir in nuts. Divide mixture in half. Evenly press half into pan bottom to form a crust. Stir baking soda, cinnamon, and salt into remaining crumb mixture until blended, then make a well in the center.

In a small bowl, lightly beat egg with sour cream an vanilla until smooth. Add to flour mixture, stirring just until combined. Fold in apples. Evenly spread batter over crumb mixture.

Bake until a cake tester inserted into center comes out fairly clean, about 1 hour and 20 minutes. If top gets too brown before cake is baked, lightly lay a piece of foil over top for last 10 to 20 minutes of baking.

Cool in pan on a rack. Serve with Brown Sugar Sauce.

Cake keeps well at room temperature for a day. Covered, it freezes well and is easily cut while still frozen.

# Roast Beef with Coffee

## Ingredients

- 4 pounds chuck roast
- 5 cloves garlic, minced
- 1 1/2 cups prepared strong coffee
- 2 tablespoons cornstarch
- 1/2 cup water

## Directions

Preheat slow cooker to low setting OR preheat oven to 350 degrees F (175 degrees C). Using a sharp knife, make 5 or 6 deep slits around the top and side of the roast. Push the whole cloves of garlic down into the slits.

Place the meat in a slow cooker OR a 10x15 inch roasting pan and pour the coffee over the meat. Cook in slow cooker on low setting for 6 to 8 hours OR bake at 350 degrees F (175 degrees C) for 2 to 3 hours. When roast is done, remove from slow cooker OR oven, and pour the drippings into a small saucepan over medium low heat.

In a separate small bowl, combine the cornstarch and water. Mix well and add slowly to the drippings, stirring constantly. Simmer until thickened.

# Cranberry Swirl Coffeecake

## Ingredients

- 1/2 cup butter
- 3/4 cup white sugar
- 2 eggs
- 2 cups all-purpose flour 1/2 cup sour cream
- 1/2 teaspoon salt
- 1 teaspoon baking powder
- 1 teaspoon baking soda
- 1 teaspoon almond extract
- 1 (16 ounce) can whole cranberry sauce
- 1/2 cup blanched slivered almonds
- 3/4 cup confectioners' sugar
- 1 tablespoon warm water
  1/2 teaspoon almond extract

## Directions

Preheat oven to 350 degrees F (175 degrees C). Grease and flour one 9 inch tube pan.

Cream butter or margarine adding sugar gradually. Add eggs one at time. Beating with an electric mixture on medium speed. Mix together flour, baking soda, baking powder, and salt. With electric beaters on low speed add flour mixture alternately with sour cream to butter mixture, ending with flour mix (do not overbeat). Stir in 1 teaspoon of almond extract.

Put a layer of half the batter in the pan the bottom of the pan, than a layer of whole cranberry sauce (1/2 the can). Repeat once more with the remaining batter and cranberry sauce. Sprinkle slivered almonds on top. Bake at 350 degrees F (175 degrees C) for 50 minutes. Remove from pan after slightly cooling. Drizzle glaze on top.

To Make Glaze: Mix together confectioners' sugar, warm water, and 1/2 teaspoon almond extract.
Drizzle over top of cake.

# Cinnamon Coffee Ring

## Ingredients

- 1 cup butter or margarine, softened
- 2 3/4 cups sugar, divided
- 4 eggs
- 2 teaspoons vanilla extract
- 3 cups all-purpose flour
- 2 teaspoons baking powder
- 1 teaspoon baking soda
- 1 teaspoon salt
- 2 cups sour cream
- 2 tablespoons ground cinnamon 1/2 cup chopped walnuts

## Directions

In a mixing bowl, cream butter and 2 cups sugar. Add eggs, one at a time, beating well after each addition. Add vanilla; mix well.

Combine the flour, baking powder, baking soda and salt; add to creamed mixture alternately with sour cream. Spoon a third of the batter into a greased and floured 10-in. tube pan. Combine the cinnamon, nuts and remaining sugar; sprinkle a third over batter. Repeat layers twice.

Bake at 350 degrees F for 65-70 minutes or until toothpick inserted near the center comes out clean. Cool for 10 minutes before removing form pan to a wire rack.

# Toffee Coffee Cake

## Ingredients

- 1/2 cup butter or margarine, softened
- 1 cup packed brown sugar 1/2 cup sugar
- 2 cups all-purpose flour
- 1 cup buttermilk
- 1 egg
- 1 teaspoon baking soda
- 1 teaspoon vanilla extract
- 3 (1.4 ounce) bars chocolate English toffee candy bars, chopped
- 1/4 cup chopped pecans

## Directions

In a mixing bowl, blend butter, sugars and flour; set aside 1/2 cup. To the remaining butter mixture, add buttermilk, egg, baking soda and vanilla; mix well.

Pour into a greased and floured 13-in. x 9-in. x 2-in. baking pan. Combine chopped candy and pecans with the reserved butter mixture; sprinkle over coffee cake.

Bake at 350 degrees F for 30-35 minutes or until a toothpick inserted near the center comes out clean. Cool on a wire rack.

# Coffee Liquor Chocolate Cheesecake

## Ingredients

- 12 ounces cream cheese 1/2 cup white sugar
- 3 eggs, room temperature
- 3 (1 ounce) squares milk chocolate, coarsely chopped
- 7 tablespoons heavy whipping cream
- 2 tablespoons coffee flavored liqueur
- 1/2 cup whipped cream
- 1/2 (1 ounce) square semisweet chocolate, grated

## Directions

Preheat oven to 300 degrees F (150 degrees C). In a mixing bowl blend cream cheese and sugar until smooth. Beat in the eggs, one at a time. Mix in 3 tablespoons whipping cream and the coffee-flavored liquor. Pour into an 8 inch glass pie pan.

In a small saucepan, melt the chocolate with remaining 4 tablespoons whipping cream. Drizzle chocolate in a spiral pattern over filling. Stir lightly with tip of table knife to achieve a marbling effect. Set the pie pan in a larger pan with water that comes halfway up side of pie pan.

Bake at 300 degrees F (150 degrees C) until firm in the center, about 55 minutes. Cool completely and refrigerate, covered with plastic wrap, overnight.
Garnish with whipped cream piped or dolloped around edges and shaved chocolate in center.

# Rippled Coffee Cake

## Ingredients

- 1 (18.25 ounce) package yellow cake mix
- 1 cup sour cream
- 4 eggs
- 2/3 cup vegetable oil
- 1 cup packed brown sugar
- 1 tablespoon ground cinnamon ICING:
- 2 cups confectioners' sugar 1/4 cup milk
- 2 teaspoons vanilla extract

## Directions

In a mixing bowl, combine dry cake mix, sour cream, eggs and oil; beat well. Spread half of the batter into a greased 13-in. x 9-in. x 2-in. baking pan.

Combine brown sugar and cinnamon; sprinkle over batter. Carefully spread remaining batter on top. bake at 350 degrees F for 30-35 minutes or until a toothpick inserted near the center comes out clean.

Combine icing ingredients and drizzle over warm cake.

# New England Blueberry Coffee Cake

## Ingredients

- 1 1/2 cups all-purpose flour 1/2 cup sugar
- 1 tablespoon baking powder
- 1 teaspoon cinnamon 1/2 teaspoon salt
- 1 1/2 cups fresh blueberries 1 egg
- 1/2 cup milk
- 1/4 cup butter or margarine, melted
  TOPPING:
- 1/4 cup butter or margarine, melted
- 3/4 cup packed brown sugar
- 1 tablespoon all-purpose flour 1/2 cup chopped walnuts

## Directions

In a large mixing bowl, combine flour, sugar, baking powder, cinnamon and salt. Gently fold in blueberries. In a small bowl, whisk together the egg, milk and butter.

Add to the flour mixture and stir carefully. Spread into a greased 8-in. x 8-in. baking pan. Combine all topping ingredients and sprinkle over batter.

Bake at 425 degrees F for 20-25 minutes or until top is light golden brown. Serve warm or at room temperature.

# Coffee Shop Fudge

## Ingredients

- 1 cup chopped pecans
- 3 cups semisweet chocolate chips
- 1 (14 ounce) can sweetened condensed milk
- 2 tablespoons strong brewed coffee, room temperature
- 1 teaspoon ground cinnamon 1/8 teaspoon salt
- 1 teaspoon vanilla extract

## Directions

Line an 8-in. square pan with foil and butter the foil; set aside. Place pecans in a microwave-safe pie plate. Microwave, uncovered, on high for 4 minutes, stirring after each minute; set aside.

In a 2-qt. microwave-safe bowl, combine chocolate chips, milk, coffee, cinnamon and salt. Microwave, uncovered, on high for 1-1/2 minutes. Stir until smooth. Stir in vanilla and pecans. Immediately spread into the prepared pan.

Cover and refrigerate until firm, about 2 hours. Remove from pan; cut into 1-in. squares. Cover and store at room temperature (70-80 degrees).

# Coffee Cake Supreme

## Ingredients

- 1 cup butter
- 1 cup white sugar
- 3 eggs
- 3 cups all-purpose flour
- 1 tablespoon baking powder
- 1 teaspoon baking soda 1/2 teaspoon salt
- 1 teaspoon vanilla extract 1/2 cup water
- 1 cup sour cream
- 1 cup chopped walnuts 1/2 cup white sugar
- 2 teaspoons ground cinnamon

## Directions

Preheat oven to 350 degrees F (175 degrees C). Grease and flour a 9 inch tube pan. In a large bowl, cream together the 1 cup of sugar and butter. Beat in the eggs, one at a time.

Combine the flour, baking powder, baking soda, and salt, stir into the creamed mixture. Finally, stir in the water, vanilla and sour cream. In a small bowl, combine the walnuts, remaining sugar and cinnamon. Pour half of the cake batter into the prepared pan.

Sprinkle half of the nut mixture over it, then top with the remaining batter, and sprinkle with remaining nut mixture. Bake for 50 to 60 minutes in the preheated oven.
Cool in pan for 10 minutes, then invert onto a wire rack to cool completely.

# Coffee Gelatin Dessert

## Ingredients

- 3/4 cup white sugar
- 3 (.25 ounce) envelopes unflavored gelatin powder
- 3 cups hot brewed coffee
- 1 1/3 cups water
- 1 tablespoon lemon juice
- 1 cup sweetened whipped cream for garnish

## Directions

In a saucepan, stir together the sugar and gelatin. Mix in hot coffee and water. Cook over low heat, stirring frequently until the gelatin and sugar have completely dissolved. Remove from heat, and stir in lemon juice.

Pour into a 4 1/2 cup mold. Refrigerate until set, at least 6 hours or overnight. Serve with whipped cream.

# Cherry Coffee Cake

## Ingredients

- 1 1/2 cups cherries, pitted and halved
- 2 tablespoons all-purpose flour
- 2 cups all-purpose flour
- 1 teaspoon salt
- 2 teaspoons baking powder
- 1 teaspoon ground cinnamon 2/3 cup vegetable oil
- 2 eggs
- 1 cup white sugar
- 1 teaspoon vanilla extract
- 1 cup milk

## Directions

Preheat oven to 325 degrees F (165 degrees C). Grease and lightly flour a 10 inch tube pan. Place cherries in a bowl and toss gently with 2 tablespoons flour. Set aside. Stir together the flour, salt, baking powder, and cinnamon in a medium bowl.

Beat together the oil, eggs, sugar, vanilla extract, and milk until smooth in a large mixing bowl. Stir in the flour mixture until smooth. Fold in the cherries. Pour batter into prepared pan.

Bake in preheated oven until toothpick inserted into cake comes out clean, about 6 minutes. Cool in pan 10 minutes, then turn out onto a serving plate or wire rack.

# Strawberry Rhubarb Coffee Cake

## Ingredients

- Filling
- 2/3 cup sugar
- 1/3 cup cornstarch
- 2 cups chopped rhubarb
- 1 (10 ounce) package frozen sliced strawberries, thawed
- 2 tablespoons lemon juice
  Cake
- 3 cups all-purpose flour
- 1 cup sugar
- 1 teaspoon baking powder
- 1 teaspoon baking soda
- 1 cup cold butter or margarine
- 2 eggs
- 1 cup buttermilk
- 1 teaspoon vanilla extract
  Topping
- 3/4 cup sugar
- 1/2 cup all-purpose flour
  1/4 cup cold butter or margarine

## Directions

Combine sugar and cornstarch in a large saucepan; stir in rhubarb and strawberries and bring to a simmer over medium heat. Cook until thickened, about two minutes.

Remove from heat, stir in lemon juice and let cool.Preheat oven to 350 degrees F (175 degrees C). Lightly grease a 9x13 inch pan.

Combine 3 cups flour, 1 cup sugar, baking powder, and baking soda in a large bowl. Cut in butter until mixture resembles coarse crumbs. Beat together eggs, buttermilk, and vanilla in a separate bowl. Stir egg mixture into flour until just moistened.

Spoon two-thirds of the batter into prepared pan; evenly spread on the cooled filling, then cover with remaining batter. In a small bowl, combine 3/4 cup sugar and 1/2 cup flour, and cut in butter until the mixture resembles coarse crumbs; sprinkle over the batter.

Bake in preheated oven for 45 to 50 minutes or until golden brown. Cool on a wire rack.

# Cinnamon Apple Coffee Cake

## Ingredients

- 1 (9 ounce) package yellow cake mix
- 1 (3.4 ounce) package instant vanilla pudding mix
- 2 eggs
- 1/2 cup sour cream
- 1/4 cup butter or margarine, melted
- 2 medium tart apples, peeled and shredded
- 1/2 cup sugar
- 1/4 cup chopped walnuts
- 1 teaspoon ground cinnamon

## Directions

In a mixing bowl, beat the cake mix, pudding mix, eggs, sour cream and butter on medium speed for 2 minutes. Pour half into a greased 8-in. square baking dish. Top with apples.

Combine the sugar, nuts and cinnamon; sprinkle half over the apples. Top with remaining batter and sugar mixture. Bake at 350 degrees F for 50-55 minutes or until a toothpick inserted near the center comes out clean.

Cool on a wire rack.

# Coffee Roast

## Ingredients

- 2 tablespoons butter
- 4 pounds chuck roast
- 1 tablespoon butter salt to taste
- 1 onion, chopped
- 6 cups brewed coffee
- 2 cups canned mushrooms
- 3 tablespoons cornstarch

## Directions

Melt 2 tablespoons of butter in a large saucepan over medium high heat. Add the roast and sear on all sides until well browned; set aside. In the same saucepan, melt the remaining butter, add the salt and onions and saute for 5 minutes.

Return the meat to the saucepan and pour in the coffee and the mushrooms. Bring to a boil, reduce heat to low and simmer for 5 hours, turning meat over halfway through cooking time. To make gravy:

Remove a cup of the coffee mixture from the saucepan, combine with the cornstarch, stirring until smooth, and return to the simmering pan. Mix well, remove from heat and serve.

# Apple Pie Coffee Cake

## Ingredients

- 1 (18.25 ounce) package spice cake mix
- 1 (21 ounce) can apple pie filling
- 3 eggs
- 3/4 cup fat-free sour cream 1/4 cup water
- 2 tablespoons canola oil
- 1 teaspoon almond extract
- 2 tablespoons brown sugar
- 1 1/2 teaspoons ground cinnamon
  GLAZE:
- 2/3 cup confectioners' sugar
- 2 teaspoons fat free milk

## Directions

Set aside 1 tablespoon cake mix. Set aside 1-1/2 cups pie filling. In a mixing bowl, combine eggs, sour cream, water, oil, extract and remaining cake mix and pie filling.

Beat on medium speed for 2 minutes. Pour half into a 10-in. fluted tube pan coated with nonstick cooking spray. Combine the brown sugar, cinnamon and reserved cake mix; sprinkle over batter.

Spoon reserved pie filling over batter to within 3/4 in. of edges; top with remaining batter.

Bake at 350 degrees F for 40-45 minutes or until a toothpick inserted near the center comes out clean. Cool for 10 minutes before removing from pan to a wire rack.In a small bowl, combine glaze ingredients. drizzle over cooled cake.

83

# Overnight Coffee Cake

## Ingredients

- 3/4 cup butter, softened
- 1 cup sugar
- 2 eggs
- 2 cups all-purpose flour
- 1 teaspoon baking soda
- 1 teaspoon ground nutmeg 1/2 teaspoon salt
- 1 cup sour cream
- 3/4 cup packed brown sugar 1/2 cup chopped pecans or walnuts
- 1 teaspoon ground cinnamon
- 1 1/2 cups confectioners' sugar
- 3 tablespoons milk

## Directions

In a large mixing bowl, cream butter and sugar. Add eggs, one at a time, beating well after each addition. Combine the flour, baking soda, nutmeg and salt; add to the creamed mixture alternately with sour cream. pour into a greased 13-in. x 9-in. x 2-in. baking dish. In a small bowl, combine the brown sugar, pecans and cinnamon; sprinkle over coffee cake.

Cover and refrigerate overnight. Remove from the refrigerator 30 minutes before baking.
Bake, uncovered, at 350 degrees F for 35-40 minutes or until a toothpick inserted near the center comes out clean. Cool on a wire rack for 10 minutes.

Combine confectioners' sugar and milk; drizzle over warm coffee cake.

# Cocoa Coffee Milkshake

## Ingredients

- 2 cups vanilla ice cream
- 1 cup milk
- 1 teaspoon vanilla extract
- 1 tablespoon instant hot chocolate mix
- 1 tablespoon instant coffee granules

## Directions

In a blender, combine ice cream, milk, vanilla, hot chocolate mix and instant coffee. Blend until smooth.

Pour into glasses and serve.

# Cranberry Swirl Coffee Cake

## Ingredients

- 1/3 cup chopped walnuts 1/2 cup butter or margarine, softened
- 1 cup sugar
- 2 eggs
- 1 teaspoon almond extract
- 2 cups all-purpose flour
- 1 teaspoon baking powder 1/2 teaspoon baking soda ½ teaspoon salt
- 1 cup sour cream
- 1 (16 ounce) can whole berry cranberry sauce, divided GLAZE:
- 3/4 cup confectioners' sugar
- 2 tablespoons milk
- 1/2 teaspoon vanilla extract

## Directions

Sprinkle walnuts into a greased 10-in. fluted tube pan. In a mixing bowl, cream butter and sugar. Add eggs, one at a time, beating well after each. Stir in almond extract.

Combine the dry ingredients; add to creamed mixture alternately with sour cream. Spread half of the batter over walnuts. Top with half of the cranberry sauce. Repeat layers. Bake at 350 degrees F for 50-55 minutes or until a toothpick inserted near the center comes out clean. Cool for 10 minutes before removing from pan to a wire rack to cool completely.

In a small bowl, combine glaze ingredients until smooth; drizzle over cake.

# Cinnamon Coffee Cake II

## Ingredients

- 1 (18.25 ounce) package yellow cake mix
- 1 (3.4 ounce) package instant vanilla pudding mix
- 1 (3.4 ounce) package instant butterscotch pudding mix
- 4 eggs
- 1 cup water
- 1 cup vegetable oil
- 1 cup packed brown sugar
- 1 tablespoon ground cinnamon
- 1 cup chopped walnuts

## Directions

Preheat oven to 350 degrees F (175 degrees C). Grease a 9x13 inch baking pan, or a 10 inch Bundt cake pan. In a medium bowl, stir together the cake mix, vanilla pudding mix, and butterscotch pudding mix.

Add the eggs, oil and water, mix until well blended. In another bowl, stir together the brown sugar, cinnamon and nuts. Pour half of the batter into the pan, spread evenly. Sprinkle with half of the nut mixture.

Cover with the rest of the batter, and sprinkle with the rest of the nut mixture. Bake for 20 minutes in the preheated oven, then turn the oven down to 325 degrees F (165 degrees C) and bake for an additional 35 to 40 minutes.

# Hazelnut Crumb Coffee Cake

## Ingredients

- 2 tablespoons all-purpose flour 1/4 cup packed brown sugar
- 2 tablespoons cold butter or margarine
- 1/4 cup finely chopped hazelnuts BATTER:
- 1 (1 ounce) square semisweet chocolate
- 1 cup all-purpose flour 1/2 cup sugar
- 1/2 teaspoon baking soda 1/4 teaspoon salt
- 1/2 cup sour cream
- 1/4 cup butter or margarine, softened
- 1 egg, beaten

## Directions

In a small bowl, combine the flour and sugar; cut in butter until crumbly. Stir in nuts; set aside. In a small saucepan, melt chocolate over low heat. Stir until smooth; cool. In a small mixing bowl, combine the flour, sugar, baking soda and salt.

Add the sour cream, butter and egg; beat until well mixed. Remove 1 cup of batter; stir in chocolate. Spread the remaining batter into a greased 8-in. square baking dish; spoon chocolate batter over the top. Cut through batters with a knife to swirl. Sprinkle with reserved nut topping.

Bake at 350 degrees F for 35-40 minutes or until a toothpick inserted near the center comes out clean. Cool on a wire rack.

# Cranberry Upside-Down Coffee Cake

## Ingredients

- 2/3 cup packed brown sugar 1/3 cup butter
- 1 1/4 cups cranberries
- 1/2 cup chopped pecans
- 1/2 cup butter, room temperature 3/4 cup white sugar
- 2 eggs
- 1 teaspoon vanilla extract
- 1 cup sour cream
- 1 1/2 cups all-purpose flour
- 1 1/2 teaspoons baking powder
- 1 teaspoon baking soda
- 1/2 teaspoon ground cinnamon 1/4 teaspoon salt

## Directions

Preheat oven to 350 degrees F (175 degrees C). Wrap the outside of a 9 inch springform pan with aluminum foil to prevent leaking. Sift together the flour, baking powder, baking soda, cinnamon and salt. Set aside. In a saucepan over medium heat, combine brown sugar and 1/3 cup butter.

Bring to a boil, then pour into bottom of springform pan. Sprinkle with cranberries and pecans. In a large bowl, cream together the butter and 3/4 cup sugar until light and fluffy.

Beat in the eggs one at a time, then stir in the vanilla. Beat in the flour mixture alternately with the sour cream. Pour batter into prepared pan. Bake in the preheated oven for 60 minutes, or until a toothpick inserted into the center of the cake comes out clean. Cool in pan for 10 minutes, then invert onto serving platter and carefully remove pan. Serve warm.

# Coffee Lover's Dessert

## Ingredients

- 10 large marshmallows
- 1/2 cup brewed coffee
- 1/2 cup whipping cream, whipped

## Directions

In a heavy saucepan, combine marshmallows and coffee; cook and stir over low heat until melted. Remove from the heat and cool to room temperature. Fold in whipped cream. Spoon into individual dessert dishes. Chill.

# Amazing Pecan Coffee Cake

## Ingredients

- 2 cups all-purpose flour 1/4 teaspoon salt
- 1 tablespoon baking powder
- 1 cup butter, softened
- 1 cup sour cream
- 1 1/2 cups white sugar
- 2 eggs
- 1 tablespoon vanilla extract
- 1/2 cup brown sugar
- 1 cup chopped pecans
- 1 teaspoon ground cinnamon
- 2 tablespoons butter, melted

## Directions

Preheat oven to 350 degrees F (175 degrees C). Line a 9x13 inch pan with aluminum foil, and lightly grease with vegetable oil orcooking spray. Sift together the flour, baking powder, and salt; set aside.

In a large bowl, cream the butter until light and fluffy. Gradually beat in sour cream, then beat in sugar. Beat in the eggs one at a time, then stir in the vanilla. By hand, fold in the flour mixture, mixing just until incorporated. Spread batter into prepared pan.

To make the Pecan Topping: In a medium bowl, mix together brown sugar, pecans and cinnamon. Stir in melted butter until crumbly. Sprinkle over cake batter in pan.

Bake in the preheated oven for 30 to 35 minutes, or until a toothpick inserted into the center of the cake comes out clean. Let cool in pan for 10 minutes, then turn out onto a wire rack, and remove foil.

# Cranberry-Hazelnut Coffee Cake

## Ingredients

- 1 3/4 cups cake flour
- 1 teaspoon baking powder
- 1 teaspoon baking soda 1/2 teaspoon salt
- 3/4 cup unsalted butter
- 1 1/2 cups dark brown sugar
- 4 eggs
- 2 1/2 teaspoons vanilla extract
- 1 teaspoon ground cinnamon 3/4 cup whole milk
- 1/4 cup dried cranberries 1/4 cup chopped toasted hazelnuts
- 1/3 cup dark brown sugar 1/4 cup white sugar
- 1 teaspoon ground cinnamon

## Directions

Preheat oven to 350 degrees F (175 degrees C). Butter and flour a 9 inch springform pan. Sift together the flour, baking powder, baking soda and salt; set aside.

In a large bowl, cream together the butter and 1 1/2 cup sugar until light and fluffy. Beat in the eggs one at a time, then stir in the vanilla and 1 teaspoon cinnamon. Beat in the flour mixture alternately with the milk. Fold in cranberries and hazelnuts. Pour batter into prepared pan. Mix together 1/3 cup brown sugar, 1/4 cup white sugar, and 1 teaspoon cinnamon; sprinkle over cake, and swirl through the batter.

Bake in the preheated oven for 75 to 80 minutes, or until a toothpick inserted into the center of the cake comes out clean. Allow to cool.

# Cinnamon-Raisin Coffee Cake

## Ingredients

- 2/3 cup sugar
- 1/2 cup vegetable oil
- 2 eggs
- 1 teaspoon vanilla extract
- 1 1/2 cups all-purpose flour
- 1 teaspoon baking soda 1/4 teaspoon salt
- 1 cup plain yogurt 1/2 cup raisins
- TOPPING:
- 1/2 cup walnuts, chopped
- 1/3 cup packed brown sugar
- 2 teaspoons ground cinnamon

## Directions

In a mixing bowl, beat sugar, oil, eggs and vanilla until smooth. Combine flour, baking soda and salt; add to the sugar mixture alternately with yogurt. Stir in raisins. Pour half of the batter into a greased 9-in. square baking pan. Combine topping ingredients half over batter.

Top with remaining batter and topping. Cut through batter with a knife to swirl the topping.

Bake at 350 degrees F for 30-35 minutes or until a toothpick inserted near the center comes out clean. Cool on a wire rack.

# Chocolate Chip Coffee Cake

## Ingredients

- 1 cup butter or margarine, softened
- 1 1/4 cups sugar
- 2 eggs
- 1 1/4 cups sour cream
- 1 teaspoon vanilla extract
- 2 1/2 cups all-purpose flour
- 1 teaspoon baking powder
- 1 teaspoon ground nutmeg 1/2 teaspoon baking soda FILLING:
- 3/4 cup chopped pecans 3/4 cup miniature semisweet chocolate chips
- 1/3 cup sugar
- 1/3 cup packed brown sugar
- 1 1/2 teaspoons ground cinnamon 1/2 teaspoon ground nutmeg

## Directions

In a large mixing bowl, cream butter and sugar. Add eggs, one at a time, beating well after each addition. Add sour cream and vanilla; mix well. Combine the flour, baking powder, nutmeg and baking soda; add to creamed mixture just until combined (batter will be stiff). Place half of the batter in a greased 13-in. x 9-in. x 2-in. baking pan.

Combine the filling/topping ingredients. Sprinkle half over batter. Spread remaining batter over top. Sprinkle with remaining filling/topping.

Bake at 325 degrees F for 40-45 minutes or until golden brown. Cool on wire rack.

# Vietnamese Iced Coffee

## Ingredients

- 4 cups white sugar
- 4 cups water
- 3/4 cup instant coffee granules
- 2 tablespoons vanilla extract
- 4 cups vodka

## Directions

In a 3 quart saucepan over medium heat, combine the sugar and water. Bring to a boil, reduce heat, and simmer for 10 minutes. Remove from heat, stir in instant coffee, and allow to cool.

When cool, stir in vanilla extract and vodka. Pour into clean bottles. Close bottles tightly, and store in a cool dark place.

# Cornish Hens with Coffee Liqueur Sauce

## Ingredients

- 1/2 cup coffee flavored liqueur 1/4 cup fresh orange juice
- 1/2 teaspoon fresh lemon juice
- 1/2 teaspoon prepared mustard
- 1/4 teaspoon ground paprika
- 3 tablespoons unsalted butter
- 4 Cornish game hens
- salt and pepper to taste
- 2 slices orange, halved
- 2 slices lemon, halved
- 1 cup seedless grapes (optional)

## Directions

Preheat oven to 375 degrees F (190 degrees C). In a small saucepan, stir together the coffee liqueur, orange and lemon juices, mustard and paprika. Add butter and bring to a boil. Once boiling, lower heat and simmer for 1 minute. Remove from heat, cover and set aside.

Rinse hens under cold running water and pat dry. Season the cavities with salt and pepper to taste. Stuff each bird with half aslice of orange and half a slice of lemon. Stuff grapes into the cavity if desired. Spoon in about atablespoon of the sauce. Truss orskewer the legs together and placebreast side up in a shallow roasting pan, and tent loosely with foil.

Roast for 30 minutes in the preheated oven. Remove foil and baste with the coffee liqueur sauce. Continue roasting for an additional 30 minutes, basting a few more times.

Remove hens to a servingplatter and remove trussing or skewers. Place roasting pan onto the stovetop and deglaze with the remaining basting sauce.

Simmer until thickened, then spoon over roasted hens. Garnish with remaining lemon and orange slices.

Lightning Source UK Ltd.
Milton Keynes UK
UKHW022110110621
385375UK00002B/227